About the playwright

Kirsty Budding lives and works in Canberra as a theatre producer and teacher. A graduate of the Australian National University, Kirsty was selected to attend the 2014 Australian Theatre for Young People's National Studio for Australia's top 20 playwrights under 25. In 2015 she was a playwright in the Fresh Ink program in Adelaide. Kirsty has been shortlisted for the Sydney Theatre Company Young Playwright's Award (2008) and has won the Canberra New Playwright's Award (2008); the Canberra Area Theatre Award for Best Original Work (2014); and the Short+Sweet Festival Best Script Award (2016). More recently, Kirsty was a semi-finalist in the 2017 ScreenCraft Short Screenplay Contest, Los Angeles. Kirsty has previously had work published in *The Voices Project: The Encore Edition* anthology by Currency Press, Sydney. For updates on her work, head to www.kirstybudding.com.au

PAPER CUTS

PAPER CUTS

Comedic and satirical monologues
for audition or performance

KIRSTY BUDDING

Blemish Books ■ Canberra

First published 2017 by
Blemish Books
GPO Box 1803
Canberra ACT 2601, Australia
www.blemishbooks.com.au

A previous version of "Bitch" appeared in *The Voices Project: The Encore Edition* anthology by Currency Press, Sydney.

Cover design by Sengsavane Chounramany (www.sengsavane.wordpress.com).
Photos by Greg Gould.

ISBN: 978-0-6482198-0-4

A catalogue record for this book is available from the National Library of Australia

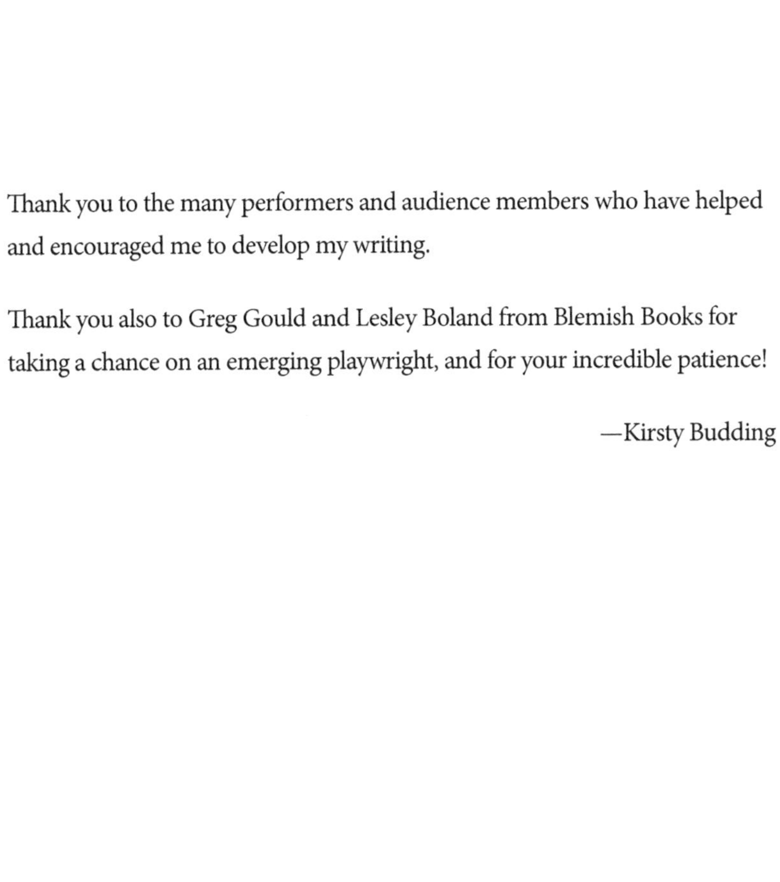

Thank you to the many performers and audience members who have helped and encouraged me to develop my writing.

Thank you also to Greg Gould and Lesley Boland from Blemish Books for taking a chance on an emerging playwright, and for your incredible patience!

—Kirsty Budding

Contents

Introduction

by Cate Clelland

Kirsty Budding has contributed a great deal to theatre in Canberra over the past few years: through her theatre company Budding Theatre; her theatrical events—especially Christmas shows; her drama classes; her work with children; her support of the work of other writers; and, particularly, her own writing of plays both short and full-length.

Now she offers a new and highly practical contribution in the form of a collection of monologues for actors and performers.

The selection offered by *Paper Cuts* provides a tool for actors who are preparing an audition piece, for those wanting a performance piece, and also for those wanting to explore character or to develop and hone their narrative skills.

The book offers a range of monologues for adults, with selections suitable for both males and females and for a wide range of ages—from young adults to the over sixties. There's something for everybody.

The wide range of subject matter includes personal relationships (predicably enough), everyday situations, and more fanciful scenarios. The subtitle "Comedic and satirical monologues" gives us a pretty clear idea as to the nature of most of the pieces. Most of them are indeed amusing—if not downright hilarious. The satire is sometimes very biting.

While many are rooted in realism and present familiar situations, others are more fanciful—even bizarre and quirky. All are well-observed, and occasionally poetic.

I recommend this book as a valuable tool for actors and performers—but also for the reader with no theatrical aspirations who might like to be entertained by these amusing and witty snapshots of contemporary life.

Enjoy!

GERTRUDE'S SWEETHEART

♂, 65+

I met Gertrude at the bingo. She'd lost her glasses and couldn't see her numbers; I was the lucky man who got to help her guide her pen. Every time my hand brushed hers, she giggled like a sixteen year old. Made me forget I was in a retirement home. I was so happy; I couldn't bring myself to tell her that her glasses had been on her head the whole time.

The next morning, I walked down to the corner shop to buy her some flowers. I thought of her giggle every step of the way. But by the time I got back to the residents' lounge, the seat next to her was taken.

It was Mr Willoughby—that smooth-talking Lothario from 29a. He's a retired British officer who wears a tweed suit and has the straightest back I've ever seen. Hardly any arthritis. He sounds like David Attenborough and he can dance—not just a slow dance; he can do the twist, the jitterbug, the tango.

He's next to Gertrude telling jokes and she's giggling away, saying, "Oh Mr Willoughby, you are funny!"

Cad. *(Confiding a secret)* Last year, there was a scandal involving Willoughby and Mrs Smith from 28a. That's right: Mrs Smith. Mr Smith was in the rehabilitation wing recovering from a hip replacement and Willoughby was ready to provide comfort, if you get my meaning. No one was surprised when Mrs Smith died of a heart attack; it was the most action she'd had in thirty years.

Then there was Mavis. And Betsy. And Doris. All decided they wanted a happy ending. I tell you: with Willoughby around, "assisted dying" has taken on a whole new meaning.

And now he was after my Gertrude! Well, when I was young, I'd have walked away. But I'm old enough to know if you love someone then you should just bloody tell them. I wasn't going to let him take her back to his parlour without a fight! So I shuffled over, holding my flowers like a schoolboy, and I said:

"Gertrude. I'm old and I can't dance and it took me an hour to get you these flowers from the corner shop, which is 400 metres away. I have a crooked back and I don't sound like I narrate nature documentaries for the BBC, but I love you.

"I can also assure you that your life expectancy will be significantly higher if you choose me. So, if you want a few minutes of excitement followed by a heart attack, then Willoughby's your man. But if you want someone who will wear you down gradually over a number of years before you finally die peacefully in your sleep, then take these flowers, and be my sweetheart."

Willoughby sneered, but Gertrude giggled and took the flowers. Then she took my arm—and as we left the lounge like two teenagers off to the pictures, she whispered:

"I knew the glasses were on my head."

Oliver Baudert OBE in "Gertrude's Sweetheart"
Photo by Hannah Baudert

MOTHER TO AN ADULT DAUGHTER

♀, *50+*

Sit yourself down! It's been weeks; why do you never visit your mother? Always working, working. Cup of tea? Are you hungry? Are you sure? You're looking thin. Are you ill? Look at those skinny hips. Need to get some meat on your bones!

How's Jonathon? Still doing a PhP? Sorry, PhD. What's it in again? Oh, that's right, poetry. That'll get him a good job won't it! *(Laughs)* So, what's his job going to be, a Doctor of Poetry? Just make sure he doesn't get up on an aeroplane when they ask if there's a doctor on board! Not the same thing, is it? Because one's useful.

Your father came up with a cracker yesterday! Do you want to hear it? What's the difference between a PhD in poetry and a roast chicken? … One feeds a family! *(Laughs)*

(Suddenly serious) You do want a family, don't you. Because you know I've been knitting baby clothes since you were twenty-five. Obviously that was some years ago so I had to expand to toddler clothes, and then school-age clothes. I've just finished the year six range.

I don't know the gender but I've been assuming it will be a girl … you know, because of Jonathon. But I've done the odd blue thing just in case you have the boy first and the girl second.

Two children: a boy and a girl. A pigeon pair! Can't have one child: they get spoilt, or strange. Can't have three or four: then you can't buy the family pass at theme parks. And we'll need that when your father and I take them to Disneyland.

Did you know that fertility declines rapidly in your thirties? I'm not pressuring you darling! I just want you to be aware that every day, your eggs are going stale. You know how your Father sometimes forgets to put the milk back in the fridge and then it goes all lumpy? That's what's happening to your ovaries. Take my advice: put a few in the freezer while they're still fresh.

Speaking of which, I've got a nice casserole defrosting in the kitchen. You are staying for dinner, aren't you?

GYM SELFIES

♂

This *(Indicating self)* is a normal body: average height, average build, stomach a bit pudgy but not fat, and arms that can easily lift everyday items and one end of a sofa if required. This body type's always been normal, alright. In ancient Rome, most guys walking around would have looked just like this.

But something's changed in the last few years. Suddenly guys need arms the size of tree trunks and pecks that dance and calves like the Hulk. I can't open Instagram or Facebook without seeing gym selfies. And even though I know it's dumb, I'm tired of feeling like the smallest guy in the bar … like a hobbit surrounded by muscular elves.

So I'm at a gym for the first time, or gYm as Homer Simpson would say, getting a fitness evaluation from a six-foot monster called Pablo. I don't know how many steroids Pablo takes, but I'm fairly sure he's going to die of a heart attack.

(As Pablo) How often do you exercise, bro?

(Trying to sound macho) Every day, bro. Four times a day.

(Pablo) Oh yeah? What do you do?

I walk. I walk to my car, I walk from my car. Then I repeat that again when I leave work.

Pablo pulls a face that actually makes him look like the Hulk. Then he drops his clipboard, and the torture begins.

(Begins exercising) He makes me do squats, box jumps, dead lifts, burpees, suicides, and other exercises with unappealing names.

(Exercise pace increases) My Kmart joggers are drenched in sweat but I'm determined to hold my own. I will not give up! With every movement, I feel myself gaining confidence. I'm not going to be the weedy nerd in the corner anymore; I'm going to be strong. I'm going to change my life. I'm going to lift weights and have muscles and wear tank tops that are too small so that everyone sees my nipples! I repeat a mantra in my head: I am not a hobbit! I am an elf! I am a sexy elf! I am Legolas!

Then I feel all woozy and my hearing goes funny and I start seeing black spots that get bigger and bigger. The next thing I know, I'm sprawled on the floor and Pablo's bottle-feeding me Powerade. There's a circle of fit dudes standing around us, their giant hands barely covering their wide grins.

A few hours later, I see my sprawled, passed out form being cradled like a baby as the backdrop of countless gym selfies. After reading a few of the comments and realising I'm never going to get a girlfriend, I do what any normal guy would do in this situation.

I log out of Facebook, turn on the TV, and cry through a nine-hour marathon of *The Hobbit*.

RUNNING INTO THE EX

♀

Oh! Hi Mark. Wow, it's been … how many years? Four. God. How have you been?—

(Quickly) 'Cause I've been fine. I mean I was bankrupt for a while after paying the legal fees to refinance our apartment; and I struggled in my work because there was a two year gap in my CV from when I devoted my life to you; and I underwent a couple of years of counselling to re-build my self-esteem after you decimated it; but apart from that—

Is this your girlfriend? Wow. You're really pretty. Amazing boobs. They jump right out at you, don't they! My boobs were always too small for him. And my thighs too big. Voice too loud—

Don't call security, Mark. Your girlfriend and I are bonding. She looks so happy, like I was when I first met you. Have you started isolating her from her friends yet? Pressuring her to stop doing what she loves?

No, you look like you're in the honeymoon phase. You have no idea, do you? All you see is his cute face and his floppy brown hair. Reminds you of a boy band, doesn't it? But don't buy it, OK. This guy's Dorian Gray. In an attic somewhere, there's a portrait of him with maggots crawling out of it.

A word of advice: don't forget who you are and what you want. Watching him play video games may seem romantic when you're in love, but do it for years and then look at what you've achieved. Look at what's left of your dreams. And even on that day, when you realise it was all about him, he'll still care less about you than where his next meal is coming from.

Anyway, I won't keep you lovebirds! Enjoy the rest of your shopping. They've got some great discounts on self-help books.

THE DIRECTOR'S NOTES

♂ | ♀

So, this is it. Opening Night. We've rehearsed for three months and, uh, well—we can't do much about it now. How do you all feel? … Good? Really? After that dress rehearsal?

I just wanted to chat to you before the show because a lot of work has gone into this. A lot of blood, sweat and tears. And I wanted to tell you that, whatever happens on stage tonight, even if the production is a disaster … it will not be my fault. I wash my hands of this production as I would wash them after petting a feral dog.

With this in mind, here are my notes from the dress rehearsal.

(Refers to list) Joseph, you missed your cue. Again. How hard is it to remember that when the Angel Gabriel—Billy, I'm looking at you; I've never seen such a bland interpretation of an archangel—when the Angel Gabriel exits, that's your cue to kneel down and look up at the sky.

And when you kneel after Mary has elbowed you and made it clear to the whole audience that you forgot your cue, can you please remember to kneel in profile rather than with your back to the audience?

And that goes for all of you. If you're speaking to the back of the stage or the floor or your hand, for some reason, Wise Man Number One, then the audience can't hear you. And let's face it, they can hardly hear you anyway. You have a diaphragm people. Use it.

(Refers to list) Props! I don't recall the baby Jesus receiving the gifts of gold, frankincense and a hand full of nothing! Where is your myrrh, Wise Man Number Three? I don't want to hear excuses; just get your act together.

(Refers to list) The closing song. I don't know where to begin. You seem to have all forgotten how to move, how to smile, and how to sing. ENERGY! I want to see wide eyes! I want to see joy at the resurrection of the saviour!

If you don't seriously lift your game, I'll make an announcement over the PA telling the audience to Google a video of paint drying to keep them entertained for those four appalling minutes.

The only thing that surpasses the closing song in lack of coordination is the final bow. What the fuck was that? When you all walk onto the stage, in a line, you need to wait for everyone to be on stage before you start bowing! Why have I got angels and farm animals bowing all over the place when the Wise Men are still filing on? I've told you a hundred times, you have to wait for the leader in the centre to bow, which is Sebastian.

Sebastian, you were only given this role because you're tall, not because you have any talent. Do not start bowing until everyone is on stage.

(Refers to list; becomes sincere) Thank you to the cleaners. Rob and Wendy. You've done a wonderful job cleaning up after rehearsals. If only the performers were as thorough with their lines as you are with your vacuums. *(Claps)* Clap everyone! Show your appreciation for the cleaners.

Now, get backstage. Your parents will be arriving soon.

SKYPE

♂ | ♀

(Talking on the phone) OK, Nan. Press the "On" button.

It's the button that's round and has the power symbol. A circle with a line. See it?

OK great. Now, wait for it to start-up. You should see a screen that has your username on it. I set your username as Florrie. There's no password so just move the mouse … the white thing on the square foam thing—move that and click on "log in."

Well done. Alright, now you'll probably see the antivirus program start up. You don't need to do anything with that, OK, so just close the window.

Nan? Did you hear me? Nan? …

Where did you go? Nan, I meant close the window on the computer. How would it help to close the living room window? How would I even know it was open?

It doesn't matter. Close the window on the computer. I mean, click the X in the top right-hand corner. Done that? OK.

Now go to the start menu—it's in the bottom left-hand corner. You'll see a space that says, "Type here to search." I need you to click in that box and type in "Skype." S-K-Y-P-E.

Are you typing it, Nan?

(Waits)

The "S" is on the middle row of the keyboard, on the left. Next to the "A". The "K" is on the same row on the right. The last three letters are all on the top row.

(Waits for an awkwardly long time)

Do you see it come up? Skype? Click on it. Is it opening? Alright! I'm going to call you. Hold on a minute.

(Hangs up phone call then looks at the phone to video call)

Hi, Nan! Can you see me? I can see you! Or I can see your forehead, at least. And the ceiling. It's like magic, isn't it!

See, now isn't this easier than using the phone?

DON'T LEAVE ME

♂

Please don't leave me. Please. I can't live without you.

No, really. I can't live without you. I don't know where you keep the food. Or the clean towels. Or the iron. Oh shit, I can't iron! I wear shirts every day! What am I going to do now? I can't believe you're being so selfish.

(Beat) I take that back. You want me to appreciate you, right? Oh! Oh, look at this apartment! It's so tastefully decorated! With all your smelly soaps and candles and your wall signs—look at this one! "Home is where the heart is". Awww. And this one: "Never take things for granted". See that's cute. Now, why would you want to leave someone who appreciates your interior design skills?

(Beat) Fine. I'll find someone else. Don't worry about me. I'm above average height and I've got a job so I'm a catch. Yep, a pretty eligible Bachelor. They'll probably ask me to go on *The Bachelor*. Sophie Monk would definitely choose me.

(Beat) I'm so sorry, I didn't mean that. I don't want anyone else! I don't want to date again! I hate dating!

I don't want to have to go on Tinder and spend ages narrowing down the options to someone who's out of my league but still achievable due to some kind of childhood trauma, then meet up for drinks, then hide who I really am for the next six months; being a gentleman and paying for dinner and acting like I'm interested in all her girly problems!

I want to stay with you, in this long-term boyfriend zone, you know? Where I can just be myself and you have to love me anyway.

Wait! Where are you going? This is your last chance. Don't you slam that door! Hey! You're walking out on true love!

(Door slams; he gets out his phone and starts swiping right)

THE HONEST ESTATE AGENT

♂ | ♀

Welcome guys! Come in! Come in!

So this is the kitchen. You may have noticed it seems a tad smaller than in the photo on the website; that's because we shot it with a wide-angle lens. We also photoshopped out the mould you can see there on the ceiling. If you do buy the place, I don't recommend breathing in this room.

Through here is the living room. As you can see, the current owners have no taste. I mean, what is this colour? Is it pink? Is it maroon? I don't know. But that's all pretty cosmetic. You could paint this a nice neutral colour and remove the fireplace and replace the floor and the light fittings and it would still be depressing because the ceilings are too low.

Bedroom is off the lounge room; unit was obviously planned by an idiot. As you can see from the chew marks on the door frame and the stains in the carpet, the owners have dogs. I don't know how many but I assume from the stench that there are enough to pull a sled.

Would you like to see the bathroom? Honestly, you don't. It's brown. Everything's brown. The bath. The sink. The carpet. The walls. The tiles are actually cream; it's just the rust that makes them look brown. Um, don't look in the toilet bowl; you'll find much the same colour scheme.

Utility room. Washing machine is included in the sale. Doesn't work.

And finally, the garden! It features an expansive five square metres of concrete overlooking—actually just looking directly at a wall. But if you put out some nice pot plants I'm sure you'll hardly notice the cigarette butts being dropped on you from the balcony above.

So that's everything. This property is in high demand due to its convenient city location, inviting offers over half a million. Would you like to take a flyer?

PLEASE ACCEPT MY RESIGNATION

♀

Dear Mr James Calwell,

Please accept my resignation from my position as Assistant Accountant at Calwell and Sons Ltd, effective today.

Thank you for the opportunities you have provided me over the last three months. In particular, the opportunities to expand my experience outside of my formal accounting role through my additional duties to prepare coffee, clean the kitchen and replenish the toilet roll. In my university study, I had not realised the importance of these domestic skills in an accounting context.

Moreover, thank you for teaching me to develop a thick skin. I now understand that the routine comments about my appearance and the puns referring to me performing sexual acts with one or more of your team were meant in good humour. Although I initially expressed concerns about being asked if I preferred a spit roast or a double-pounder, your explanation that my appearance was too distracting and that I ought to dress more conservatively if I wish to be respected made perfect sense. I now understand that men are powerless to control their natural impulses and that the onus is on me in this regard.

Although I am moving on, I hope that my contributions to meetings will support the ongoing development of the company. While you will be unaware of these contributions because you spoke over them, they were recorded in the minutes that I typed and stored on your hard drive. I trust you will have a chance to review them when you realise the illegalities in your current system, which will undoubtedly result in your arrest when the auditors arrive after the anonymous tipoff they received this morning. Apologies that my soft, female voice was unable to draw your attention to this issue sooner.

If I can be of any help during the transition, please do not hesitate to ask. I will be more than happy to provide context to the person who will replace me.

Sincerely,

That Moody Bitch with the Fine Ass

Madeline Woods in "Please Accept My Resignation"

Alexander Castello in "Love Thy Neighbour"

LOVE THY NEIGHBOUR

♂ | ♀

Look, I'm a Christian. I believe in love thy neighbour and all that. But the fact is, Christianity says marriage is between a man and a woman. That's in the Bible and the Bible is God's word. There's no flexibility; we can't just change our attitudes based on the fashions of the day.

(Thinks) Apart from burning people for witchcraft; we don't really encourage that anymore … And massacring Jews and … torturing heretics; that's frowned upon these days.

And condemning people who suggest that the earth revolves around the sun; Galileo may have been on to something there.

And slavery: bit embarrassing that we were on board with that for hundreds of years! But the Abolitionists were Christians too so, phew.

Oh, and literalism; we don't apply that reading nowadays—not to the weird parts of the Bible at least. I mean, how could two of each animal fit on an ark? Wouldn't the lions have eaten the sheep?

But apart from that, you won't find us budging on moral issues any time soon. Nope. Solid as a rock.

THE SMITTEN SCIENTIST

♂

I have to tell you. I've run all this way to tell you that I'm so in love with you. I can't stop thinking about you. It's awful. I can't get any research done. The lab's a mess. Nothing's growing in the petri dishes. I was fine before I met you and now I'm just … incomplete.

So, marry me? No. Too soon. We should probably go on a date first. My research indicated that several dates are customary prior to discussing a long-term relationship. I don't mean to assume that you would say yes; in fact, I'm aware my odds are roughly equivalent to the odds of discovering alien life within the next ten years, but I've planned for every eventuality.

I may be misreading your non-verbal cues, but you seem confused. I'm sorry; I swear I did everything I could to avoid this moment. I tried giving up coffee and walking a different way to work and throwing myself into my research but god … your face. The way you wipe steam off your forehead when you're frothing milk. The way you shake chocolate onto my mocha. The way you say, "Mocha for John" even though my name's Ron.

And your smile; you smile with your eyes even when you're not smiling. Every night I lie in bed staring up at the ceiling and I see your smile. Sometimes you wave down at me, like this *(Waves)*.

And I keep imagining the scene of us getting together; we make love right over there next to the napkin dispenser.

I shouldn't have told you that. It's not just physical. You're perfect in my eyes, both biologically and in the sense that you have a beautiful soul. The soul isn't real, biologically; I just mean that you're a good person. I'm trying to be romantic because, according to the internet, women like that.

Helen—I hope your name badge is accurate—Helen, when I first saw you, I finally appreciated the wonders of science. Evolution took place just so that one day, someone as beautiful as you could exist. The laws of physics; gravity itself seems to have been designed with the sole aim that you might one day fall into my arms. And penicillin wasn't discovered by accident; Alexander Fleming wanted to make sure that I wouldn't lose you to a bacterial infection.

But over the past few weeks, I've also felt the limits of science. Because I can't rationalise this. I can't quantify or measure it. And I'll never be able to talk about my feelings for you in cold, objective language. I'm biased and it feels amazing, and I'll gladly produce skewed results for the rest of my life if it means I can spend it with you. The controlled variable, the thing that will never change, is my love for you. But without you, I'm just a hypothesis.

I'm trying to be romantic. Is it working? I assume so as you seem to have been rendered speechless, along with all your patrons.

… I don't really know what to say now … dating etiquette baffles me and the advice I got on Reddit was very confusing, but here goes:

Helen, would you like to have a coffee with me?

JUST BROWSING

♂ | ♀

Hi, how are you going? Can I help you find anything today?

No, you're just browsing. OK, there's no need to be a bitch about it. A smile wouldn't kill you. I hate my job and I'm still smiling. You think I want to ask people if they need help just to get rejected every time? It's in my contract.

It's also in my contract to re-fold that sweater that you just scrunched up while you were looking for a size 12. I could have told you there were no size 12s. Now the display's a mess.

Do you know how many sweaters I fold every day? How many dresses I hang up because some dickhead knocked them off and walked away? It makes my fingers hurt. Thanks to you, I'm one step closer to rheumatoid arthritis. In fifty years, I'll have trouble opening doors and turning on taps. I probably won't even be able to afford medicine because my retail superannuation will be so shit. But it's OK because you're JUST BROWSING!

(Regains composure and customer service manner)

Just give me a shout if you need anything.

ALEKSANDR

He came in carrying a leather suitcase and staring deep into my eyes. Then he said, "Good morning" and I thought, oh god, he's Russian.

What is it about Russian men? The way they stare at you, unafraid, daring you to drink vodka and forget everything. The way they do things with their tongues that English speakers just never learn. He could be reciting his shopping list—"eggs, milk, bread, toilet paper"—and I'd still hear "Let me take you back to Mother Russia and we'll go and see Chekhov plays every night … and I will give you massages, also."

Aleksandr was like a kitten—a Russian Blue with startling eyes. In the evenings, he curled up on my lap and everything was so warm. So sexy, yet so innocent. Nothing mattered any more—not day or night, convention or tradition; it all disappeared in a snow storm of romance. We listened to Tchaikovsky and he read aloud from Tolstoy; and with every heavy, rolling R, I fell more in love.

Of course, there were some who thought our relationship was not entirely appropriate. I was called in to explain myself. I tried to tell them that I didn't mean for it to happen; that he was the one who did the chasing. I mean, he literally chased me around the bedroom pretending to be a bear. Grrrrrrr.

They stared at me, all grey and disapproving in their suits, like I was some fallen woman of the 19th century.

Don't look at me like that! Don't you understand that we're in love? I'm the Anna Karenina to his Count Vronsky!

At this point, the Headmistress leaned forward and said: "Mrs Brown, given that he's your son's foreign exchange student, I feel a more appropriate analogy would be that you're the Humbert to his Lolita."

Well, I haven't read *Lolita*, but I've seen the movie with Jeremy Irons and I can assure you that Aleksandr is not a child. What is age anyway? It's just a number. Forty-one. Seventeen. Just numbers. And it will be good for him! A relationship with an older woman is a character forming experience! He could become the President of France now! Or Russia. I suppose Russia. In any case, he's more of a man than any middle-aged man I've ever known. And far better in bed.

The women of the school board squeaked like scandalised nuns: "Enough, Mrs Brown! Do you really not understand how irresponsible you've been?"

Of course I know that. I'm a mother. I'm over forty. I know this is hardly role model behaviour.

But … have you ever put your hand on your heart and imagined it not beating? Don't you wake up every morning knowing that you're one day closer to that moment? To non-existence; to being a memory in someone's head that will last a few decades and then disappear, because you won't have any great Russian novels to leave behind.

Have you never wanted to just drink vodka and forget? Forget that you're getting older. Forget about all the things you wish you'd done. Forget about your nine-to-five job and your responsibilities.

Have you never had a person stand in front of you, who made you ask the question: why am I alive, if not to live?

They shook their heads, and I left quietly with the police.

THE CEO

♂

What do you mean you've lost it? It's a 1.4 metre novelty cheque for a hundred thousand dollars! How the hell could you lose it?

I don't think you understand how serious this is. I'm supposed to present a giant cheque to the Children's Charity in ten minutes. We've done a media call. We've booked photographers. And worst of all: we've organised two children to accept it. Two orphaned children. They've been excited about it all week. And now you're telling me that the CEO of the Commercial Bank is going to hand over a normal-sized cheque to two crying children?

This is a major boo-boo. This is worse than that time you forgot to pick up my dry cleaning and I had to give a speech to the board in my Hawaiian shirt. You had two weeks to pick up that dry cleaning while I was in Honolulu. Two weeks!

I'm sorry but I'm going to have to look for a new personal assistant. Please make a note that you need to write an advertisement for your job.

Now pass me my cheque book. *(Holds out hand; waits)*

You don't have it, do you. *(Beat)*

Fine. Get me a piece of paper. It'll have to be an IOU.

I HAVE A DREAM, CAROL

♀

So she said to me: "You can't wear that skirt to work. It's inappropriate."

Inappropriate how, Carol? Inappropriate because we live in a shallow society that judges people based on their appearance, and the judgements are framed within a patriarchal discourse in which women are either the Madonna or the whore; a respectable woman or a slut? Is that why, Carol?

She rolled her eyes: "It's unprofessional."

Oh! It's unprofessional. Well, now I'm confused. Am I a bee-keeper? A firefighter? A trouser model? Because my profession chiefly involves sitting at a desk, using my brain to transmit messages to my fingers to tell them to type documents for this god-forsaken organisation. Is my skirt going to reduce my capacity to do that? Will it change the composition of my brain? Break the connections between my synapses? Cause my hypothalamus to melt?

"This is not up for debate."

Not up for debate? Carol, I fear you may be overlooking the urgency of the moment. You know why? Because I have a dream, Carol. I have a dream that one day, a woman will be judged not by the length of her skirt, but by the content of her character. I have a dream today!

I have a dream that one day, even in the corporate world, with its vicious sexists, with its middle management dripping with the words of "inappropriate" and "unprofessional"—one day women with short skirts and women with unflattering suits like yours will join hands as sisters.

I have a dream today!

At this point Carol, fearful I would paraphrase all of Martin Luther King's "I Have a Dream" speech, interrupted with, "Fine, just wear the fucking skirt!"

I smiled sweetly, climbed down from my desk, and said: "Thanks Carol; I'll have these documents typed and on your desk by the end of the day."

CONSERVATIVE DATE

♀

(A well-groomed woman enters a bathroom. Her face and hair are wet. She grabs paper towels to dry herself and spends the rest of the monologue re-applying her makeup in the mirror — the mirror is the fourth wall between herself and the audience.)

So I'm having dinner with this idiot and after three courses and much intellectually-barren conversation, he looks at me over his crème brûlée and says:

"You're a nosy whore. Go fish for compliments elsewhere."

Well, I didn't know quite how to respond. I had merely enquired about the fiscal health of his dental practice and made a throw-away remark about the virtues of teeth whitening.

Calmly, I replied: "First of all, I am not nosey; I'm inquisitive, like Sherlock Holmes—except I don't deduct anything but my own opinions.

"Secondly, I am not a whore. If I were, you would be paying several thousand dollars for my company since, had I not been blind drunk when I agreed to this date, that is the only way you would attract someone of my calibre.

"Finally, I don't need to fish for compliments; they jump out and slap me in the face. If it seemed I was fishing for compliments, it was only my attempt to offer gentle reminders of how lucky you are to be here, lest you should regret your ungentlemanly behaviour several years hence as you sit in a rundown rental property with your fat fiancé, who you will never actually marry, eating KFC and shouting because you can't hear the television over the sound of your dyslexic children."

He looked at me with the same horrified expression he'd worn since I ordered the lobster.

Then, and you won't believe this, he took his glass of water, and he threw it in my face. The man threw the drink at me, a woman.

Have I fallen down the rabbit hole? Am I in a parallel universe?

You know who I blame? Feminists. As soon as they started complaining about men opening doors for women, I knew that would be the end of civilised society. It was a slippery slope then to women paying half the bill and then taking it in turns—there is nothing more unromantic than equality.

If God wanted us all to act the same, he would have made us asexual. Men want sex which, ultimately, makes women go into labour. If men want sex then they must also labour, through door-opening and bin-carrying and shopping and paying and listening!

And now he's gone! Without paying! I would have offered to pay, trusting he would do the gentlemanly thing and refuse.

Apparently, some women get a kick out of wining and dining men; I've never understood that. Men should be protectors, providers; it doesn't matter that women can afford it now because we're not in the fifties. This isn't about economics. It's about romance.

You know why I'm really angry? It's because life was simpler back then. Now everyone's so confused. Is it romantic or politically incorrect? Sexism or chivalry?

Chivalry is by definition sexist; that's why it's so great. And romance isn't politically correct because the heart doesn't give a shit.

I want silly traditions. I want someone to take charge, because I'm tired of being in charge. Life is so full of sensible reality; of ruthless fairness—it's exhausting. Can we not keep this one silly illusion alive, so that a woman feels special for one evening in her dreary working life?

I suppose I better go pay the bill.

UNWANTED GIFTS

♂ | ♀, 60+

On top of my shelf, there's an answering machine, still in its box; a food processor with the cord still wound up; and a coffee maker that's never made a cup of coffee. I keep the display in the hopes that my relations will get the hint.

Every year they ask what I want for my birthday and I say, "a pair of socks." They laugh and say, "We can't get you socks! We have to get you something nice!" So they get me the latest gadget; meanwhile my socks are full of holes and I'm running out of shelf space.

And that's a parable for our time, isn't it? Can't just get me what I want. Oh no. You have to get me what everyone else wants. What the ads on TV say I should want. Some machine that will do a function that I can either do myself, or that I don't want! I can make my own coffee. I don't need a food processor because I already own a revolutionary utensil called a knife. And I'm retired with a phone next to my armchair so if I don't answer, it's because I don't want to talk to you!

The last thing I want to do is trawl through messages saying, "Are you alright? Have you had a fall?" or "You have to be careful at your age," or "Have you updated your will recently? Because I just wanted to let you know that I like that ring you wear on your little finger."

Young people think buying things will make life easier; they don't understand that the easiest life is a simple life, without any of this internet … computer … Bluetooth … nonsense.

Fortunately, I've got a plan. Because I thought to myself, they're never going to buy me anything that isn't an electronic gadget, correct? So next time they ask, I'll be ready. I'll say:

"For my birthday, I'd like a top-of-the-range, Bluetooth-enabled, electric sock-maker."

HAIRSPRAY ISLAND

♂

I've been staring at the bathroom door listening to my wife's grooming rituals for two and a half hours. Are we going somewhere special, you might ask? Is it a wedding? A party?

Oh, no. She decided today she wanted to buy some solar lights for the garden and maybe some book shelves for the bedroom. That's right. She's spent two and a half hours getting ready to go to Bunnings.

(Calling to her) Rachel! Hurry up! And please stop playing Ed Sheeran!

She always gets annoyed when I complain, like I'm the unreasonable one. Like I should just eternally amuse myself while she's straightening her hair and listening to "Thinking Out Loud" on repeat. If I have to listen to—*(Imitates Ed Sheeran)* When your legs don't work like they used to before *(Stops)*—one more time, I'm going to … *(Searching for a harsh punishment)* I'm going to pace up and down this hallway looking put out.

(Paces for a time) Look! It's almost two o'clock! We probably won't even arrive in time for the sausage sizzle! It's been four hours since breakfast! I'm wasting away! *(Falls to his knees in despair)* I feel like I'm stranded on a desert island and it smells like hairspray. It makes my throat hurt … *(Rasping)* water … By the time Rachel's finished her makeup, I'll look like Tom

Hanks in *Castaway*. I didn't think I'd ever experience anything slower than that movie. Or I'll be like Bear Grylls, drinking my own pee after filtering it through a sock.

These song lyrics don't even make sense! Why will he only love her until she's seventy? Is he just going to dump her when she's seventy-one? I hate Ed Sheeran so much, that romantic little ginger git—OH MY GOD THE DOOR IS OPENING!

(Quiet awe, with a hint of romance) And there she is, stood in the doorway. Is she really ready to leave, or is it a mirage? No, that's definitely Rachel.

(Slowly rises to his feet) But I'm speechless, because she looks perfect. I look her up and down and I think to myself: no matter how long it takes her to get ready, she'll always be worth the wait, and I'll be waiting long after she's seventy. I take a deep breath, and I say …

(Incredulous outburst) Is that all?! It took you two and a half hours to brush your hair and put on a pair of jeans! You'd look the same if you'd only spent ten minutes in there! I've been waiting for two and a half hours! My stomach's rumbling! And I got all the stars in Angry Birds! All of them! Didn't you say you wanted to get solar lights?! And maybe a book shelf?!

Rachel looks confused. "Yeah," she shrugs, picking up her keys. "But who said I wanted you to come?"

Brenton Cleaves in "The Law Student"

THE LAW STUDENT

♂ | ♀

Torts. What does that even mean? It's such a strange word. It sounds like 'totes.' You know, like totes boring or totes hard, or totes high rates of suicide in the legal profession. The only thing I learnt in Torts was the phrase *res ipsa loquitur*—and I have no idea what it means.

I think we can all agree that most students who study law have no interest in law. Mummy and daddy just want to tell their friends about their successful kid because a high-paying career equals success and successful kid equals successful parents, right?

(Imitates a posh woman's voice) "Oh, dahhhrling, we're so delighted! John's at Sydney studying law! He's going to be a barrister! Oh, and next year, Clara's going to study medicine!"— even though John's a prick who spends all his time getting drunk because "Ps get degrees," and Clara's depressed because the only way she'll ever touch a dick is by examining one to check for herpes.

So these poor, rich kids enrol in law or some other degree society told them was prestigious, but then there's a snag. They actually have to do it. They have to read law textbooks and write dull essays and this time their private school teachers aren't there to spoon feed them the answers. And sooner or later, they'll realise that:

Number one: they're not that smart.

Number two: they can't change the world or international law or any other grandiose idea they got from doing a forty-hour famine in their multi-million-dollar school gym.

And number three, that every single year in Australia there are more law graduates—more aspirational, talentless clones graduating—than there are actual legal jobs in existence at any point in time.

Then they'll give up, go out and get drunk, come to a lecture hungover, and make a speech that they might regret after the Panadol kicks in.

And that, ladies and gentlemen of the jury—or lecture theatre —is how I know that the defendant's alibi is a piece of shit, because no law student would be sitting alone in their room studying Torts on a Friday night.

THE MODERN FAIRYTALE

♀

My husband's so desperate for sex, he'll interpret the slightest thing as a signal that I'm interested: spooning, cuddling, wearing a nightie, making eye contact.

To avoid any awkwardness, I try to make my intentions clear. I get into bed wearing a dressing gown over a onesie over Bridget Jones underwear. I casually mention that I've had an upset stomach lately because of some bad curry. And if I feel obliged to touch him, I pat him on the arm the way I would pat a feral cat in Bali. Then I roll over like, *(Yawning)* "I've got an early start in the morning." *(Fakes snoring)*

It's sad because in the beginning, it was like a fairytale. He swept me off my feet and I couldn't get enough. All I wanted to do was marry him and live happily ever after.

But now … he makes this annoying sniffly noise in bed. I mean, he doesn't blow his nose; he just sucks it up. His pillow is covered in drool and he mutters about spreadsheets in his sleep.

Meanwhile I'm fantasising about Ryan, the twenty-six year old EA who just started working in my office. Why would I want to have sex with my husband, when I can imagine Ryan bending me over my ergonomic chair?

I suppose we'll get divorced, eventually, and join the list of all the failed marriages of our friends. All the weddings we've attended together; all the happy photos that are flaunted for a couple of years and then hidden forever when things go wrong. I don't even enjoy weddings anymore because I know how the story ends.

Except it doesn't really end, does it. We just get bored a few chapters in and want to start again. Because beginnings are more exciting than the middle, aren't they. Why continue through the boring bits when you can start again?

Once upon a time, there was a handsome Prince called Ryan, and a much older, divorced Princess …

SEX WITH MOLLY

♂

(Henry enters carrying a pot plant. He puts it on a table and contemplates it.)

Sex with Molly was surprising. I don't mean it came as a surprise; I knew it was happening. I don't mean it was surprising because of how it was, either; you know, the style or the ins and outs of the thing, which were—meh. It was because I'd always thought of Molly as asexual.

I met her in a gender studies lecture even though I was there for commerce and that was awkward. She sat next to me wearing a sort of shapeless cardigan thing and no shoes. She spoke like she was speaking in her sleep—vague and dreamy. I walked out with her mainly because I thought she looked lost, even though I was the commerce student who'd just sat through gender studies 101: the history of men being cunts.

I dunno what it was about her; she wasn't my type. She read poetry all the time; not even proper poetry—that sort of vague "found words" sort of poetry; the collected scribblings of some dead folk-singing homeless person who was too stoned for the discipline of metre. Hints of ideas but nothing concrete. I can't stand things that are open to interpretation. If you're going to leave everything open to interpretation, you might as well not write and let people write something themselves.

Create meaning or don't fucking create.

Molly wasn't a creator; she was a thinker—the kind who's highly analytical and intelligent but who lacks discipline. Her thoughts ran faster than her reason, or the ability of her sleepy voice to keep up, so that profound sentences trailed off into the mumblings of a drunk.

But here she was, that abstract collection of drunk words and barely-thought thoughts, colliding with something concrete. Hard.

Like I said: the sex wasn't great. She just looked bewildered; sometimes indifferent; maybe curious? I thought I saw pleasure at one point but then realized it wasn't related to my dick; I think her mind was elsewhere. She wasn't inanimate exactly, more … otherworldly or *(The plant)* like a plant. She was like that in general—this floaty thing tied to the earth. Natural and unsatisfying, like her diet.

Molly's a vegan. When we ate out, my meals made her cry and think of lambs. She hated violence; a steak knife was barbaric. She'd look at me over the table with these big, infuriating eyes and say: "Henry, animals feel pain too."

I'd say: "But they lack intelligence. They're bred for our consumption. They wouldn't exist without us. It's a food chain. It's evolution. It's survival. They eat each other so why can't we eat them. You think a lion wouldn't eat you, you daft hippy?"

(He picks up a watering can and waters the plant)

She got me this plant. Said I should learn to take care of a living thing other than myself. Think she was calling me selfish.

Guess who she votes for? *(The plant)* The Greens. Can you imagine? The upper middle-class commerce student from the Liberal-supporting family of lawyers with the lower middle-class daughter of an impoverished musician and an anaemic feminist.

Political Liberals don't fuck philosophical liberals. It just isn't done. We move in very different circles and her circles are fucking nuts.

She took me to a poetry slam once. Oh. My. God. While she enjoyed it, I sat in the corner writing my own poem on my phone. Here. *(Looks through phone)* I showed it to Molly saying I wanted to get up and perform it but she wouldn't let me, so I'll perform it now.

It's called "Poetry Slam". Ahem.

> I'm at a poetry slam
> It's basically a hipster rant
> It looks like a man with a beard
> Rounded up every unpopular kid
> And made him wear a waistcoat.
> It's cute how you think waistcoats are cute.
> I like the op-shop chic and ugly girls complaining
> About misogyny to mask self-loathing;

It's so hip.

Your poems are hip too

Pretentious as they are predictable

Social justice, down with racism and uni fees! Your
thesis is:

Everything would be better if the world were run by
bright young things like us!

Liberal-minded, sensitive souls who see beyond the
shallow masks of men

Sorry, the shallow masks of humans

You don't like gendered language. Gender is a construct;

Everything is a construct,

Including you and your fucking poems.

But you wouldn't know a half rhyme

If it jumped up and fucked you from behind.

And the irony—you love irony—is that I agree with you

On every point

But you smell like marijuana and poverty

And contribute nothing to society

So get a proper job and—

(Molly enters wearing nothing but a smock)

Uhh—Molly! I didn't know you'd woken up. You look good.
Nice … dress? Can I get you something? Non-dairy soy chai
latte with a sprinkling of no flavour?

(Molly walks up to the plant and strokes its leaves)

Oh, good, petting the plant. Giving it the morning stroke. That will definitely help it grow.

(Molly lifts up the plant to reveal it has been over-watered)

You told me to water it! Now you're mad that I drowned it. Well guess what? You're drowning me! I can't live on a diet of soy milk. I need steak and sausages and—sense! Make sense!

Poetry should rhyme or at least have some artistic merit. If women want high positions, then they should work for them; don't expect us to reserve you a job just because you've got a vagina. Lions eat people. Oh! Oh! You defend people who belong to intolerant, sexist, racist religions and cultures to prove you're not intolerant, sexist or racist. How do you think that's gunna work out for you? Freedom is an illusion—no one would really like it if they had it because we like boundaries and if you destroy every tradition on earth you're destroying history and then what's the point of anything and—

(Molly kisses him, then suggestively takes his hand and pulls him towards the exit. Helpless to resist, Henry's last line is all he has left—)

The Greens will never form government!

DISTURBED DANCE INSTRUCTOR

♀

Hi everyone! Are you ready to get fit? Are you ready for Sh'bam?

I'm really sorry if you are because I didn't actually get the license and their moves are copyrighted!

So today I'm going to teach my own original dance fitness routine! On your feet! Let's go! *(Claps)* First let's step side to side. *(Step side to side)* Great job! And now the Dad dance! *(Dorky dance).* Awesome! Now drunk girls in the club! *(Messy drunk dance)* Now vain girls in the club! *(Self-conscious, pouty, barely dancing dance)* OK, let's change it up! Checkout chick! *(Checkout operator dance moves)* That's right! Bag up those groceries! Now kid having a tantrum in aisle three because his mum wouldn't buy him lollies! *(Dramatic tantrum on floor)* Now mum crying into her wine because motherhood isn't fulfilling! *(Crying into wine routine)*

And now my husband with my next-door neighbour when I'm not home because he doesn't know about the secret camera! *(Kissing and sex dance which gets increasingly disturbing)*

Alright, let's take five.

AUNTY AUSTEN

♀

My Dear Madam,

It is a truth universally acknowledged that, no matter how accomplished a lady is, when she is trying to decide whether she should break up with her boyfriend, she will Google it.

This truth is so well-fixed in Google's algorithms that Google knows the question before the lady has finished typing it. She need only type "should I b"—just the letter B—before she sees the following options in order of popularity:

Should I break up with my boyfriend?

Should I buy a mac?

Should I buy a house?

Hello, I'm Jane Austen. You may remember me as the author of such classic literary hits as *Pride and Prejudice*, *Sense and Sensibility*, and to a lesser extent, all the other novels I wrote. Although I never married, and the concept of a carnal relationship outside of marriage is unpalatable to my late 18th to early 19th century sensibilities, I am here to save you from the Wickhams and Willoughbys of the twenty-first century.

Let us begin. Ahem.

Obviously you should break up with him because you are asking Google.

This is a clear indication that you know the answer but you do not trust yourself. I understand it is usual for ladies in these situations to seek advice or to create a "pros and cons" list. For example, pro: we both enjoy reading, dancing and playing the pianoforte; or con, when he touches me I feel nothing, as if my lady flower has shrivelled up and died.

As I have often noted, a marriage without passion cannot be agreeable to either party. The thought makes me more depressed than the casting of Keira Knightly as Elizabeth Bennet in *Pride and Prejudice*, when Jennifer Ehle clearly defined the role in the 1995 BBC adaptation.

Of course, it is possible that the lack of physical attraction is mutual and that this is acceptable to both parties, in which case you may simply be elderly or infirm. However, if you lack amatory inspiration, try roleplay.

(Imitates sexy roleplay voice) Oh Mr Darcy! / Oh Lizzy! / You are tolerable I suppose, but—/ Oh shut up and take me!

(Regains composure) Let me advise you that writing a pros and cons list is quite foolish for, as I demonstrated in Mr Collins' hopeless proposal to Lizzy, love is not a business proposition. A lady who is truly in love would never dream of listing the cons of her soul mate.

Perhaps he is cruel or dishonourable; perhaps he is proud, or even prejudiced. Or perhaps he is perfectly agreeable, but he is just not your Mr Darcy.

It is not his fault, and you cannot explain why, but you know in your heart that something is missing. You fantasise about a room of one's own; independence. The freedom to do what you are meant to do.

I never married, though I had many chances … alright I only had one chance. But still, if I had married, I would not have had time to write. I may even have died in childbirth at a young age, instead of reaching the ripe old age of thirty-seven. I would not have been able to write some of the most popular and adored works of English literature. My refusal to conform has led to generations of people remembering my name; and yet my contemporaries who bore children to carry on their names, are forgotten.

I bet Google didn't think about that.

This, madam, is a faithful narrative of my views on your unfortunate circumstances.

Your role model,

Jane Austen

Postscript. You should not buy a mac. They are most displeasing.

Post-Postscript. It is excellent that ladies are now able to own property. You should purchase an estate if the conditions are favourable, to wit: a good-sized deposit, reasonable interest, and a positive forecast for growth in the area. Otherwise, you will spend years paying rent to assist someone else to pay their mortgage, leaving you with no assets when you are an old spinster, thus forcing you to enter a workhouse.

BEACH BLUES

♂ | ♀

I don't want to be here; my family made me come. "You have to get out more!" I wish they'd get out more—out of my face.

I hate the beach. Nothing but expensive ice cream, hot sand that burns your feet, sharks that want to eat you, and loads and loads of ridiculously attractive people.

I mean, look at him! What are you, Wolverine? And look at her! She's hotter than Jessica Alba circa 2005. I'm glad I'm wearing reflective sunglasses because I can't stop staring. All the flat stomachs and abs are making me want to cry, and then comfort myself with food. When I see bodies like this in magazines, I always tell myself they're photoshopped, like, "That's unrealistic! People don't really look like that!" Then I come to the beach and I realise: nope, I'm just ugly. The only thing melting faster than my Cornetto is my self-esteem. It's basically a puddle now.

They must have spent months planning this; like, they would have needed at least a few weeks to train, or to recover from the surgery. And to plan the outfits! Look at these perfect, colour-coordinated beach ensembles and accessories accentuating their hotness.

(Mimicking) "Oh, look at me! Look at my defined arms! Look at my designer beach towel! Look at my beach hair! I wear sea salt spray in my hair even though I'm next to the

fucking sea!" They think they're so cool with their personal trainers and their willpower.

All I've got is my Coles brand factor 50 and a SpongeBob towel I've had since primary school. Yep, it's like school all over again, and I'm still the pasty loser who the cool kids don't want to play with.

Ah well. Fuck it; I'm gunna build a sand castle.

Glynis Stokes in "Beach Blues"

THE PRINCIPAL'S ADDRESS

♂ | ♀

Alright settle down, settle down. I know you're all keen to go home, but it's important that in assembly we are attentive and respectful until the very end.

As your new Principal, I have been delighted with your behaviour in the first week back. I know it can be a difficult transition from the school holidays to morning classes, but you have overwhelmingly been outstanding in your adjustment. I have only had the police called to the school grounds twice this week and just one teacher has had a mental breakdown. Give yourselves a pat on the back.

I'll keep this brief; I'd like to discuss three things today. I'll begin with a motivational talk about the sports teams, followed by some housekeeping notes on etiquette in the playground, and end with an introduction of myself as your new principal—

(Stops abruptly)

I notice as I speak that a few of you—and by a few I mean roughly ninety-nine per cent—are playing on your phones. I believe strongly in treating you like adults, which is why we don't have consequences for bad behaviour at this school, however I must insist that you put your phones away, just for a moment, please, so that you can concentrate on my positive reinforcement of your good behaviour.

(Waits for a moment, looking around)

I see that you are so engrossed in your phones that you didn't hear me, and I am in fact giving this speech to myself and the three or so students at the front who will make it to university. If you persist in not listening, I will be forced to raise my voice.

(Waits, then raises voice)

There will be consequences for phone use while the Principal is speaking! Don't push me, students. I am not afraid to make empty threats to contact your parents. That includes you, Brayden. I see you swiping up and down; loading and reloading. You don't have any Facebook notifications; no one cares.

(Responds to the audience response)

Apparently individual rebukes capture your attention. Around fifty per cent of you are now listening, so perhaps I will move on to discuss the sports teams. I feel strongly about the importance of sport and physical education to the school spirit and, given that our academic results are amongst the lowest in the country, this is all the more essential. You can sign up for sports teams by seeing Mr. Evans in the PE Office—*(Stops, as if someone is whispering in their ear)*—I've actually just been informed that Mr. Evans has gone on stress leave, so you can see Mr. Turner if you're interested in sport.

My second notice concerns the playground, and by the playground I of course mean the car park. Year eleven and twelve students with licenses must register their cars at the front office and must not invite friends from other schools to do "doughnuts" in our carpark. You are also kindly requested not to loiter in your cars or play offensive music loudly near the classrooms. I have been told that several maths classes have been disrupted by the pervasive beats of Kanye West.

(Responds to audience)

Ah, you find that funny. Though I see that I still only have seventy percent of the room. Would it help if I offered a story about my teenage experiences riding in cars in the seventies to make you realise I was young once too? My friends and I would go out in my Mum's old Ford Falcon listening to "sick beats" like "Night Fever" by the Bee Gees. Sometimes we waved at teenagers of the opposite gender. Those were wild times, I can tell you.

… Now none of you are listening. Apparently, you don't care that I used to be young—in fact it makes you respect me less. Good to know.

Fine. Well, nothing makes people listen like the truth, so here goes:

I'm the Principal and I lack principles. I didn't become a teacher because I had a calling or even because I liked children; I became a teacher because I gave up on my dreams. Now I talk convincingly at large functions about the nobility of teaching but consistently go over the heads of my teachers for nefarious and political reasons. I disapprove of discipline and academic rigour; instead, I favour a warm and fuzzy approach with abundant use of the word "community". I have low expectations of your achievement because you're at the tail-end of the socio-economic bell curve, and I'm just doing my time here before I can get a job at a private school.

And I won't miss you, because I'll see you every day when I get my drive-through coffee at Maccas.

And look at that—you're all listening! Well done. All that remains for me to say is:

Welcome. Welcome to our school community.

NOT CREEPY

♀

It's not creepy. Definitely not creepy. Lots of people stalk other people on Facebook and Instagram and … while they're jogging around the lake. It's not creepy because it's true love. I know it's true love because last time he spoke to me, I literally forgot how to talk.

So I decided next time, I'd be ready. I've prepared some friendly, casual-sounding things to say when I inevitably bump into him. "Inevitably" because I'm going to pace up and down this path until I do. It goes like this:

Oh, hey! Do you live around here too?—*(Aside)* I actually live on the other side of town, but if this works then I'll move —Yeah, I was just out for a jog—*(Aside, sneakily)* hence the Activewear—oh, do you like jogging too? Do you go jogging every evening between six and six-thirty too? Woah, coincidence much! *(Smiles)*

It's really hard to bump into someone when they're jogging at ten Ks an hour. I tried yesterday and he ran right past me. Didn't even glance. I thought about hiding in a tree and dropping from a low-hanging branch, but then I had a better idea.

(Starts hobbling and overacting) Ohhh, owww! Damn this sprained ankle that I got while I was jogging! It's so stiff and painful! I'll have to lay down in the middle of the path.

(Falls to the ground dramatically)

Help! Won't someone rescue me and carry me home? Oh the pain!

(Sprawls sexily, then peeks between her fingers)

I hear footsteps! I try to pull off pain and sex appeal all at once *(Struggles to pull a face that expresses this)* and then—wait, who is that? *(Looks into the distance, horrified)* There's a blonde woman jogging next to him! She's wearing Lorna Jane. I can tell from her athletic arms that she doesn't just exercise when she's stalking people.

I'm caught in a fight or flight response. Do I lie here and be helped up by both of them, or do I run? It's possible she's his sister, right?

I run. I run just in time to see them both looking slightly curious but they don't even slow down. They keep jogging like demi-gods as I retreat to the nearest tree and try to look like I'm stretching my calf muscles when really I'm keeling over because I've got a stitch.

But the stitch is nothing compared to the pain in my heart.

He looked like he recognised me, but not enough to say hello. He looked like the times we met didn't mean anything. All those times he came into the store and asked me where things were. Doesn't he remember the canned beetroot? How I placed it in his huge, gentle hand?

Or when he came to the register and spoke those beautiful words: "How's your day going?" He didn't have to ask. Why do people ask how people are if they don't really care?

He probably wanted the canned beetroot to make her a salad. He'll probably come in tonight to buy condoms but no lubricant because her vagina works just great without it. They'll probably run out because of all the sex, and next year I'll be bagging up nappies for their newborn.

And one day it will all get too much and I won't go to work. But he won't notice. Because I'm not the sort of person who gets noticed. I'm the—

(Turns as the good-looking man appears)

Oh, shit! Hi! You … you heard all that? The part about the beetroot and the … sex.

"Yeah," he says. "I heard everything. She's my sister. And I'm obviously not going to have sex with her."

(Trying to be cool) Yeah, cool. *(Awkward)* So … do you come here often?

ETIQUETTE

♂

Have you ever noticed how men and women segregate themselves at parties? It's not like in the olden days when it was written in etiquette books that the women had to withdraw after dinner so the men could smoke their cigars and talk about manly things like owning property and voting.

Yet here we are in the twenty-first century: the wives and girlfriends are in the corner of the bar gossiping and I'm stuck here watching the football. At least I think it's football … there's a ball. I just cheer when everyone else cheers and look disappointed when they look disappointed.

I wonder what the womenfolk are talking about. They're all smiling and joking and drinking piña coladas. I wish I could have a piña colada, but we all know what the guys will say if I order one. I have to drink beer because jugs are ten dollars and I have a penis.

This is so unfair; I'm missing all the gossip! I've got an inkling that Dave's wife Sharon is pregnant, and I overheard that her mate Angela just got a new job but her boss is a pervert, and Sarah—that's my girlfriend—she's whispering something to Joe's wife. What if she's talking about what I'm like in bed? I want to be in on that!

Nah. Screw this. A real man doesn't fear judgement. I'm going to go and sit with the women!

(Walks over) So I approach the table. They all look up at me, a little alarmed, like I'm a bear that just wandered into their secret women's cave.

"Hi ladies. I got a bit bored of football and beer so I thought I'd hang out with you. So … what are we talking about?"

They exchange awkward looks.

"It's alright, you can keep on gossiping! I'll start! What's that sound? It's the pitter patter of tiny feet, am I right Sharon?! And Angela, sorry to hear your boss is a pervert—too bad. You should report him and have him locked up. And Sarah— I hope you've been telling them I'm huge. Huge, ladies. Sometimes too big, you know, 'cause Sarah's pretty tight. Sometimes it hits the wall."

They look horrified and I realise I've failed at being one of the girls. Sarah looks like she might never sleep with me again. Abort mission! I sprint back to the football. Beer has never tasted so sweet.

On the way home in the car, Sarah tells me Sharon isn't pregnant; she's just put on a few pounds—they'd been trying to reassure her it wasn't noticeable. And I obviously misheard the thing about Angela's boss; he's not a pervert, he's apparently perfect and she's in love with him. And Sarah didn't tell them anything about me in bed because apparently women don't really do that.

But Sarah, I was only trying to break down gender barriers! I was trying to resist outdated, nineteenth-century gender norms!

She rolls her eyes and tells me to sleep on the sofa. The next morning when I wake up, there's a small booklet on the armrest written in Sarah's handwriting. The title: "Etiquette for the 21st century boyfriend, Volume 1."

A PLANT LIKE JIMMY

♀

(Recoils & screams, then relaxes) Oh, it's OK. It's just a dead leaf. Sorry. When I'm gardening, it's like 10 per cent gardening and 90 per cent checking for spiders.

I'm having a garden party; it seemed like a good idea at the time, you know, like the Queen's garden parties? Kind of posh. But to be honest, I hadn't actually been in my garden since I moved here two years ago. Turns out it's just dirt and snails back here.

So I'm planting some ferns because that's what the garden centre lady pointed to when I said I was looking for a plant like Jimmy. Obviously she was like, "Who's Jimmy?" and I explained:

"Jimmy's this guy who I'm not interested in and who I generally ignore; but every now and then I'm in a strange mood and decide I'd like Jimmy in my life for a few hours and I call him and there he is. Without fail. Last minute social events. Booty calls. Laundry. You name it. So basically, do you have a plant that I can treat like shit and it will still be there for me?"

She pointed to the ferns like she felt sorry for them.

(Continues gardening) But it's going to be great. These ferns will add a bit of colour and I'll get some string lights and mojitos and it will be amazing. There are so many cool people coming. Jimmy's not invited, obviously. What if I want to hook up with

someone else? Can't have him staring all doe-eyed and tragic from the corner. He did that at the Christmas party. For some reason, he'd got it into his head that the four hours of wild and passionate sex the night before meant we were a thing.

(Recoils) Ewww, a snail. Gross. Kinda reminds me of Jimmy. Small and vulnerable and … when you really look, kind of cute …

Man … I talk about Jimmy a lot considering I'm not interested in him at all! I don't know why. That's so random. I mean we're so not right for each other you know, because he's a dork and I'm hot and because … because he's kind and good and I'm a bitch.

(Beat; she bends down) Come on little snail. Let's find you a safe place where I won't accidentally step on you and break your heart.

DATE NIGHT

♂

Thursday night is date night—the day of the week where we get a babysitter, go and have dinner, and pretend like we're still interested in each other. It was Michelle's idea. Something about maintaining her sanity. Anyway, so this Thursday she wanted to try somewhere different.

(Imitates Michelle's voice) "I want to go somewhere nice! We never go anywhere nice! Susan's husband took her to that new restaurant that just opened overlooking the water and she had real champagne from Champagne! Why don't we ever do anything nice like that?"

I don't know what's wrong with Hog's Breath or Sizzler or the Westfield food court; but you know women always want to go somewhere a bit fancy to show off to their friends and *(Imitates)* feel like a princess.

So she insists on going to this place called "Q" she read about in a magazine. We're greeted by a French guy with a tight shirt and suspenders who's polishing a glass like it's some kind of performance art.

(Imitates waiter) Bonjour. 'Ave you been here before? Would you like me to explain 'ow eet all works?

How it all works? Apparently, I need the concept of ordering food explained to me.

(Imitates waiter) All our food and drinks are displayed on zat board so you'll 'ave to turn around to view ze menu. We don't 'ave physical paper menus because we like to keep eet simple and all about ze food which is all organic and beautiful, but not as beautiful as your wife.

(Rolls eyes) Well, Michelle's happy. She'll have someone to think about next time we have sex.

After a bit of back and forth with Pierre, I work out that "Chateaubriand on a bed of kohlrabi with a side of caramelised onion cigar celeriac purée" means something like "beef on cabbage with onion sauce."

I try to look forward to my meal. The food's twice the price of Hog's Breath so I'm expecting something huge. But when it arrives, the food on the plate is like how the earth must look from space.

I know Michelle likes all this fancy stuff so I try to relax. I don't say anything about the little green blobs and orange dashes on the plate that seem to serve no purpose. Michelle's laughing and joking around with the Frenchman. As I watch her, I realise I haven't seen her this happy since we actually went on dates, before the kids. Before the mortgage. Before we needed date night.

I pay the 240 dollar bill. I know Michelle's expecting me to wince or pull a face, so I just smile and say, "You're worth it" and her face lights up. I can tell she's gunna be telling her friend Susan all about this tomorrow, saying "It was so fancy, the waiter was French and they didn't even have menus."

And for once, I'll be that husband whose wife is showing off because for a few hours, she felt like a princess.

I'm glad she felt like a princess, because we're going to be having date night at the food court for the next ten years. 240 bucks! That's a bloody power bill! She and the kids better stop leaving the lights on from now on. Do they think there's a money tree in the garden?

240 bucks for that French nonsense. *(Shakes head)* I'd rather have fish and chips.

ENABLER

♀, *40+*

Thank you so much for calling me in! It's really lovely that Alex's teachers are keeping a close eye on him. He's such a special boy. So, what's this all about?

Absent? On which day? On Thursday. That's interesting because I dropped him at the school gates that morning. Perhaps someone marked the roll incorrectly? Alex tells me that happens all the time. He's so quiet, you see; the teachers don't notice him. You're certain? Alright, I'll call Alex to clear this up.

(Gets on phone) Alex darling! It's Mummy. Listen I'm at the school and your teacher says you didn't come in on Thursday, which I know can't be true because I dropped you—*(Beat)* Yes. *(Listens)* Ohhh, I see! Oh, you are a sweetheart. I knew there'd be an explanation. Don't worry, I'll sort it out. Oh, I bought some cheese pizzas for you and your friends. They're on the bottom shelf. OK. Love you. Bubbye. *(Hangs up)*

It's alright, Alex told me everything. He was about to enter the school gates when he saw, in the distance, an injured duck. Alex is a compassionate soul, so he followed the duck to the lake and spent the day nursing it back to health. And then the duck laid eggs and Alex is going to visit every day to help raise the ducklings, like in that film with the geese. *Fly Away Home.* You see! I knew there would be a logical explanation.

If there's nothing else—

(Listens) What do you mean, suspected drug use? Marijuana? Alex wouldn't even know what it looks like! *(Beat)* No, I was not aware that the lake is known as Stoner's Lake. But when I get home, I'll ask Alex if he saw any suspicious activity while he was helping the duck. *(Beat)* That photo proves nothing. In fact, the bloodshot eyes merely confirm Alex's story: he must have been crying all morning because of the duck.

(Rises) Thank you for calling me in. I'm so proud of him. You know, when all else fails in my life, I comfort myself that at least I got one thing right.

Joan White in "Grandma's Sex Advice"

GRANDMA'S SEX ADVICE

♀, 60+

Now dear, I know you probably don't want to hear your Grandma talking about the sticky business but I just want you to be prepared. Back in my day, people didn't talk about these things. You'd get a shock on your wedding night, I can tell you. Or a disappointment, in my case. So, I want to tell you all the things I wish someone had told me.

First, honesty is the best policy. When you're making love, don't copy porn stars and make ooooh and ahhhh noises just to boost his confidence because he'll take that as encouragement to keep doing what he's doing, and what he's doing is probably shit.

Second, beware the UTI. That's right. Urinary tract infection. Very painful. I got one on my honeymoon. It's all the bacteria getting pushed in and out. But there's a trick: have sex when you need to wee because then straight afterwards, you can wee all the nasties out.

But make sure you only need to wee a little bit. Don't have sex with a full bladder. I made that mistake once; it felt like I was being hit with a hammer.

Finally, be safe! Use protection! That's if you don't want the pitter patter of tiny feet, or the clap. Gonorrhoea is very unpleasant; just ask your grandfather. Speaking of which, if you need some condoms, there's some in his sock drawer.

Oh, I'm sorry, I've made you uncomfortable! Don't worry, we don't use them for sex! That time is over for us.

No, he uses them to spank the monkey because once he was pleasuring himself to that lovely assistant on *Countdown* and he got his sticky juice all over my nice Persian.

Fluffy's never been the same.

Anyway, don't tell mummy about our little chat. She thinks I'm going senile.

Now, be a good girl and finish your homework.

CARAVAN DREAMS

♀, *50+*

So I said to Bill, let's just do it! We're not getting any younger and I'm sick of everything. Sick of cleaning rooms that just get covered in dust again. Sick of looking after a big empty house when I've got no time to look after myself.

So let's just do it. Let's buy a caravan and drive around the country! We can cruise the coast, sleep under the stars and pop in to visit the kids when we need a hot shower. They've all made such an effort to move far away from us that we'll have a choice of destinations. It'll be romantic!

That's what I said a year ago. Now it's three AM and Bill's over there in that panel van getting stoned with two German backpackers. I can hear them singing Edelweiss; it's like *The Sound of Music* on mushrooms.

If the police come, I'm not bailing him out. This was meant to be our dream. Our twilight years. But no, it's all "chill out, Maggie" before he ditches me for Friedrich and Kurt so they can have a "jam session" on Kurt's ukulele.

Chill out! You're almost sixty, you daft git! You want to feel young again with these stoned kids? Fine. You never paid attention to me anyway. Left me out with the kids. Left me out with your friends: "Don't worry about old Maggie, she'll be right."

You know, I don't think I remember a time he ever really listened. When he was ever really present. He'd grunt when I asked him about his day. He'd nod about the house and the kids without ever knowing what he was agreeing to. He'd snore through my favourite films.

He even snored through *The Sound of Music*; I mean, what kind of monster does that? I bet he never paid attention to the bit when the nuns open their hands and reveal the wire cutters they used to damage the Nazi cars.

No, Bill. They were half way across the Swiss Alps by then.

And god, the Blue Mountains look beautiful right now.

BITCH

♀

You know when someone insults you while they're pretending to be your best friend? Jessica starts conversationally bitch-slapping me and I can see it happening like that moment in the *Lion King* when Scar reaches out to pull Mufasa from the ledge, then digs in his claws.

And I'm like, "Hey bitch. Your blonde hair extensions can't hide your black soul. These people may think you're hot, but isn't it ironic that you love taking photos of yourself because you hate yourself? Looking through your Instagram is like X-raying the *Mona Lisa* and seeing *The Scream*."

She doesn't get the art reference, just like she doesn't get me. Good. Must mean I'm more complicated than a blow job.

She clacks away in her tacky shoes and I'm alone again, calm— like I'm not touched by anyone 'cause I've given up on people. It's all a game: the social survival of the fittest. A bunch of teenagers getting drunk, showing off and following the alpha. But I'm more evolved.

Oh, my Mum's here to pick me up! Yeah, my mum picks me up from parties at ten PM because I'm a loser.

She's like, "Hi baby, how was the party? Did you and Jessica make friends?"

I'm like, "No, Mum, Jessica's a whore."

She's like, "Don't talk about your sister like that."

Then Jessica gets in the car.

(Imitates Jessica) "Oh my god, Mum, can you not make me take that antisocial bitch to parties? It's like, so embarrassing."

So we're driving to McDonalds and Jessica's going on and on about what a bitch I am. Urgh, stop exaggerating Jessica! All I did was tell everyone how insecure you are. That's not a lie, unlike your face.

Then she starts crying and mum starts fussing and it's just like when she was born all over again. Poor baby Jessica. Mum and Jessica should be the poster for co-dependency.

You know what pisses me off about Jessica? It doesn't irritate me that she's weak. It irritates me that she pretends to be strong. I don't care if she hates herself. I care that her way of covering that up is to act like she loves herself.

"Jessica, I'm sorry you hate yourself and that you're too dumb to work that out, but the truth is better than your Barbie extensions and fake eyelashes, which are coming unglued by the way, so just shut the fuck up!"

Jessica's response is to vomit on the floor of the car. It smells bad—really bad—as if the vomit is sad.

I'm not sure why I feel bad then. Maybe it's because I didn't hold back her hair and now her blonde extensions are brown … the colour her hair was once, when she was my little sister; or because she's looking into the pool of vomit and realising she's not in love with her reflection. I kind of wish she could find that pool of water somewhere where she's beautiful at the bottom.

I'm also frustrated that the drive-through lady can't hear my order over all the crying and the spewing, so I look at Jessica and decide to give her some sisterly advice.

"Jessica, do you know why people are bitches? It's because they know, deep down, that they're a bitch, and that makes them hate themselves, so they have to bitch about someone else— I mean, pretend the other person is a bitch—in order to hide the truth from themselves that they are, in fact, a bitch."

"And guess what, Jessica?" *(Gestures to herself, not Jessica)* " … You're a bitch."

She stops crying, and I let her share my fries.

THE ACTOR

♂

(With an exaggerated English accent …)

> Two households, both alike in dignity,
>
> In fair Verona, where we lay our scene,
>
> From ancient fudge break to new mutiny,
>
> Where civil blood makes civil hands … hands …

(Forgets words; takes a rolled-up script out of back pocket and reads)

Unclean! *(Does a double take)* Oh, it's grudge. *(Writes a note)*

You know what I love? The stage.

(Gets out phone) Almost as much as I love my Facebook page. My actor page has six hundred and ten likes now. I add people I don't really know—you know, people with mutual friends, people I pass in corridors—and then immediately invite them to like my actor page. It's only a matter of time before I get really big. My mentor at uni said I have the right look for Hollywood, and they know someone who knows someone who knows a casting director, so they should know.

(Starts to take a selfie, then puts the script in the selfie with him)

You know what the difference is between a professional actor and an *(Air quotes)* "actor"? Some people think it's the ability to act—WRONG. It doesn't matter if you can act well if you can't drop names into a conversation. Who was your mentor at uni? Who did you do a workshop with? Who did you see once at the deli in Coles? It was Hugh Jackman, by the way. He was buying salami.

It doesn't matter if you have a great look if you haven't had it captured by the right photographer. It doesn't matter who you are if you don't have a website, blog, Facebook page and business cards to make it real. *(Starts handing out business cards to the audience)* Call me.

Because you can't just be real; you have to be virtually real. *(Phone rings)* Some people need to get their priorities right.

(Answers phone) Alexis? Hi. Yeah, I'm well. Looking forward to the news! *(Listens; face falls—)* I didn't get it? Who did? Tom? Are you fucking kidding me? That guy doesn't even have professional headshots! Nah, nah; I'm fine. I'm fine; I'm not bitter, no. Don't worry about me. It's fine. I really feel like this play was a bit, you know, amateurish for me anyway. I mean, if they're going to hire an untrained actor over a trained one, then clearly our artistic values are incompatible. Yep, you keep me in the loop now! K, bubbye.

(Hangs up, pauses for moment and then loses it)

Tom! Fucking Tom!

(Composes himself, then calls Tom)

Tom! Hey buddy! How you doing? A little birdy told me you got the lead in that play, well done! … Oh, I heard about it from one of my contacts in the industry, you know, in the amateur scene. Former contact really because we don't have much of a reason to talk anymore. I feel like when you move in a certain league it's not good to move backwards, you know …

(Listens)

Yeah, Alexis told me; yeah she's great. Anyway, some of my mentors from acting school are hooking me up with casting agents for *Home and Away*, then I'll probably do the Hollywood pilot's season … What? The play? Nahhh, I didn't go for it. I thought about it, just for fun, you know, but my schedule's looking pretty tight in the next few weeks. Yeah, I'm working on a feature … I can't really give you the deets cause it's kinda on the D-L. The producer doesn't want to put it on Starnow or anything because they don't want every Tom, Dick or Harry who thinks they're an actor rocking up, you know what I mean, Tom? But if you want I can keep an ear out for anything that could be suitable for someone at your level. Yeah! I'll pull some strings. You can be my protégé! K. I'll see you around … oh! Have you liked my actor page? Of course you have. K, bubbye.

(Hangs up the phone, then starts a status update)

Congratulations to Tom on his new role. I have personally mentored Tom and it's great to see an aspiring actor do some amateur theatre. I'm sure my connections can help Tom develop his skills so that one day, he'll be able to star alongside a professional actor like me.

(Stops typing; puts phone away.)

In a minor supporting role. With no lines.

AWWWW

♀

So I'm sitting at my desk and suddenly all the women in the office start making "awwww" noises. My heart leaps because I know what that means. I'm already picturing the cute little face and the cuddles!

Imagine my horror when I turn around and find that it's not a puppy, but a human baby. And now that I've turned around with obvious interest, I can't just swivel my chair back again like, "Eww." I mean, the mother might get offended. So, I have to respond … but how?

I try to mimic the expressions of the other women. Have you ever noticed how your face hurts when you fake smile? The sides of my face quiver as I try to find this small, drooling human with a cone-shaped head appealing.

My colleagues are crowding around and taking it in turns to speak to the baby as if they're also babies. They pass the baby like it's the most exciting pass the parcel game and I'm terrified someone might pass it to me.

Maybe I could excuse myself to go to the bathroom … no, they're forming a wall. There's no escape. Now they're all staring at me, as if they said something but I didn't hear it because of the internal monologue.

Do I want to come and see the baby? Boy, do I.

So I walk up to the baby, surrounded by women who have, you know, feelings, and I try to mimic their response:

(Tries to say "awwww" but sounds like a goat)

Later, one of the women asks me quietly, "You know when Vicky brought in her baby, why did you make that goat sound?"

I say, "I'm sorry, honestly; I just don't know how to respond like I'm supposed to."

She puts her hand on my shoulder and whispers: "Don't worry. When I see a baby, I just imagine it's a kitten."

Cameron Thomas in "Things I Hate"

THINGS I HATE

♂ | ♀

(A person enters holding a list – deadpan, almost bored)

Here is a list of things I hate. *(Consults list)*

I hate when you're trying to find a park and you think you see one but it's actually a small car.

I hate Times New Roman, size twelve. We use it for everything but it's a really uninspiring font.

I hate it when you order a hot chocolate and it's served lukewarm.

I hate world hunger.

I hate people who don't stand to the side on the escalator.

I hate how retail workers are helpful when you're just browsing, but disappear when you need help.

I hate frost on the windscreen in winter.

I hate cyclists.

I hate *Star Wars. (Substitute for any popular film franchise that may appeal to the audience)*

(If negative audience reaction) I hate people who judge people who don't like *Star Wars.*

I hate the suffering of child soldiers.

I hate people who walk slowly.

I hate people who never get driving licenses because they say they don't need one and then they always ask you to drive them around.

I hate crying babies on aeroplanes. *(Thinks)* Actually, that's mean. *(Takes a pencil and adds a couple of words, then re-reads).* I hate the parents of crying babies on aeroplanes.

I hate cruelty to animals.

I hate overcooked steak.

I hate it when people put up those copy-and-paste statuses on Facebook. My mum gets annoyed when I don't share.

I hate it when people don't look like their profile photos.

I hate how hard it is to be authentic when everyone's pretending.

I hate brown bread. And raw sugar. And vegetables.

I hate free apps with in-app purchases.

I hate spitting in public.

I hate people who don't wave to say thank you when someone lets them in at a busy intersection.

I hate how politics attracts the kinds of people who shouldn't be politicians.

I hate reality TV.

I hate *Pop Idol* and *X Factor* and *The Voice* and *So You Think You Can Dance* and *Dancing with the Stars* and *Dancing on Ice* and any other TV talent show that celebrates the fact that talent is common and reward is rare.

I hate people who chew loudly.

I hate the immense, overwhelming mystery of life and the universe because it makes me feel like everything's pointless.

I hate advertisements with really catchy jingles that you can't get out your head. *(Sings or hums a catchy jingle)*

I hate how a corrupt banker can make more money in one year than an honest cleaner can make in their whole life.

I hate it when my laptop runs out of battery.

I hate how I'm dying slowly, every day, and I can't stop it.

I hate when the writing on a T-shirt fades after one wash.

I hate how I'm going to lose everyone I love, eventually.

I hate liquorice.

And finally, I hate it when psychologists make me articulate my feelings by writing lists of things that I hate. It's really unhelpful and look! I got a paper cut.

… I hate paper cuts.